ELDORADO

By the same author:

Yes and No (Peterloo Poets, 1979)

A Second Life (Peterloo Poets, 1982)

Jouissance (Peterloo Poets, 1985)

Editor: *Between Comets: for Norman Nicholson at 70* (Taxus Press, 1985)

Keith Douglas: a study (Faber & Faber, 1987)

Eldorado

WILLIAM SCAMMELL

PETERLOO POETS

First published in 1987
by Peterloo Poets
2 Kelly Gardens . Calstock . Cornwall PL18 9SA

© 1987 by William Scammell

All rights reserved. No part of this publication may be reproduced, stored in a retrieval system, or transmitted in any form or by any means, electronic, mechanical, photocopying, recording, or otherwise without the prior written permission of the publisher.

ISBN 0 905291 88 3

Printed in Great Britain by
Latimer Trend & Company Ltd, Plymouth

ACKNOWLEDGEMENTS are due to the editors of *Critical Quarterly*, *Encounter*, *The Honest Ulsterman*, *The Literary Review*, *London Magazine*, *New Statesman*, *Poetry Book Society Winter Supplement (1984)*, *Poetry Durham*, *Poetry Matters*, and *Poetry Review*, in whose pages many of these poems first appeared.

The author wishes to thank the Arts Council for a Writer's Bursary in 1985, and the Djerassi Foundation, California for an Artist's Residency in the same year.

WITH THE ASSISTANCE OF
SOUTH WEST ARTS

For Alan Ross,
poet, traveller, editor extraordinary.

Contents

	page
Looking for Mel	9
Route One	11
Santa Cruz	13
Three Jolly Barbers	15
Names	16
The Gatsby Variations	17
Corfu	18
First Sailing	21
Eldorado	22
All at Sea	26
Senhouse Street	27
Road Movie	29
Younger Brother	30
Der Gang Zum Liebchen	32
Coming of Age in NW3	34
The Waverer	35
The Woman Who Wouldn't Sit Down	36
Hypnos	38
The Perfect Uncle	39
Death of a Bird	40
Eclogue: Clerk of the Weather	41
Rydal Water, Winter	44
Nicola	45
To a Pink Dress	46
Boaz and Ruth	47
Outcast	50
Larkin's Dead	52
Library	54
Learning the Cello	55
Pub	56
More Bagatelles	57
Tree Heads	59
Olive and Autumn	60
Seven Smells	61
Da Capo	63
Byron's Bedroom	66
Verses	68
It's All right Ma, I'm Only Sighin'	71

Looking for Mel

Once off the freeway, nose-diving
round hairpins to cross the booming river
we took ourselves up into the Sierras,
lost in the high spaces of a noun.

Not quite trackless, nevertheless
dark with redwoods standing
from one Israel to the next.
Iowa Hill was the last outpost,

a wooden store whose grizzled prop
sat on his six-thousand-foot stool
thinking. His tin specs wished
you well, if you deserved it,

a moot point sweetly made. Yes
we were right for Mel, and crawled
slowly on up into the forest
that was his only known address.

The road gave out, and then the track.
There was a log across a path.
Evidently the PRIVATE PROPERTY—
KEEP OUT signs were aimed at us

and stray prospectors of the IRS
for this was gold country, staked out
and haunted since by men
whose only pension was an aching back.

A dog barked. There was Mel
shambling out of the trees, sculptor,
miner, mute and burly as a mole.
In forty years he'd sunk nine shafts

through solid rock, and found enough
to good as lacquer his wife's nails
if she'd still been around.
He poured the dust out

from a paper twist. It winked
a little, in his rocky palm,
then each grain faded back to sleep.
The guest-house was a dacha,

hand-built, one of several
tucked into his wild estate.
A rocking chair sat
like a modest buddha by the door.

Our bedroom smelled of pine,
must, paraffin, all happy things
to be knocked down to
at the end of the long day.

Pancakes for breakfast, a rich
breath of trees. He tossed a stone
into his flooded mine, and smiled,
and winched his shoulders straight again.

There were earthworks all around—
gardens, mineshafts, sculptured chambers
aimed at the summer solstice, where
once a year the sun might strike . . .

plans requiring another lifetime
to add to his sixty-something,
crammed with the stuff of legend
from his fighter-pilot-boyhood on.

What he scented wasn't money:
he dug the way his water-wheel
panned luscious cold new water
down by the forty-niners'

long-since-vanished flume.

Route One

Nicest of oceans, at any rate best christened,
the Pacific bowls in like a healthy child
and sprawls to rest under California's

motherly high dome of blue and gold.
Route One is our altar, laid out among
pillars of leaf and rock, wiped free

of all but expectation and the odd cyprus
dramatising its enviable grip on a site
chosen to undress in by the sun.

Carmel, Big Sur, Monterey—I am here
to inspect the far-off poetry of my bookish
teens, that can of worms... '*We are the world,*

we are the children' booms and fades
from every waveband of our automatic Tempo.
Bells chime out over Nepenthe's high plateau:

we drink our tea to a tune going nowhere,
swallowing the real and ersatz peace once bought
for Rita Hayworth by a svelte young Orson Welles.

Thousands of shock-pink Mexican crabs
have migrated this year to die on the beaches
of Monterey. A lucky few wash up

in the outside pool of the new aquarium;
others crawl high up the sand and wind slowly
down, ticking inaudibly as quartz.

The motel has a classic redwood bar—
there's even a big fight flickering onscreen
for us to eat hamburgers by—and

at 3 a.m. the waitress brings her lover in
to warm the cabin next door. Their talk
and its declensions might as well be here

drowning on our thin pillows ... or
sluicing itself off in this tin shower,
its Peter-Pan-sized thumb of soap.

Santa Cruz

Four red-tailed hawks circle and circle
above the valley, a lazy bolass
flung high over the hills of Santa Cruz.

The redwoods seem to grow in pairs
like brothers and sisters, their cones
heavy and symmetrical as grenades.

One sits on my desk now, loosening
its chain-mail in the sun, while a lizard
interrogates itself on the fence beyond.

Great white pillows of fog drift over
the Pacific, a child's view of heaven.
I've yet to see San Francisco

but I've watched the racoon who steals
up on to the verandah every night to eat
catfood and rattle the dustbins. I've seen

the great-horned owl too, and the brilliant jay
who steals so charmingly you wouldn't
even think to put him on probation.

They've promised me deer, bobcats, coyotes
and, if I don't watch out, the miseries
of poison oak. What they didn't mention was Mike,

the handyman all-rounder who squats
on one heel under the Californian sun,
tall and lean as one of his old-fashioned shovels,

watching us trying to fatten our lines.
He rounds up silence, and cooks his food
in a pit. Right now he is digging

a thin tracery of trenches outside my window
for the new sprinklers, stooped attentively
over the blond eloquence of his moustache.

Down in the circular barn Rick is painting
the huge ochre spaces of the south-west
and Rachel has three strawy shamans rowing

for dear life in pursuit of someone's soul.
Yesterday I wept at the beauty of it all
helpless in some turbulence of loss,

the lizard's frozen half-turn into stone.

Three Jolly Barbers

It's haircut time in Palo Alto.
Three jolly barbers, multiplied fore
and aft in giant mirrors, liquid tool
of the trade, are listening to the game
and calling out jokes their fathers made.
We are on Spinoza or Balzac Ave.
This is a university town
laid out like a crossword puzzle
more or less anyone could solve.
The sun is shining, the tall trees growing.

Rich in hair-splitting tautologists
the experts analyse tactics
on and off the air. The barbers snip
their scissors; as the game warms up
their combs freeze in mid-air. All three
have bellies and a belt. They move
like dancers who have danced so long
they've slowed down to vestigial movements
of the hands and feet. Each foot
is shining, each substantial arm
fits snugly in its short-sleeved shirt.

Every so often they walk
in back and front of you
like courtroom lawyers on TV,
acting themselves but with a higher good in view.

I paid my dollars, plus a goodish tip,
and wandered to a second-hand
bookshop, name of *Chimaera*, where
my whole appearance ceased, and I
grew even happier than before.

Names

There doesn't seem to be a name for that sort
of Biedermeyer, wedding-cake architecture seen in New York's
turn-of-the-century pink hotel
which pops up now and then among the canyons

like a sweet tooth, apotheosis of a certain
prosperity of bust, the ravenously slim waist.
Stepped like ziggurats, they handle accretion
with aplomb. Yellow taxis buzz in and out

and the twentieth-century revolves a little
making a modest side-stroke for the desk.
I thought of all this at the Russian party
down in the Village, where men and women

bulging with sorrow like brandy glasses
wept dry-eyed in enormous vowels
for the murderous accommodations sweeping
them in and out of art historical time.

The Gatsby Variations

Even to the layman boats are beautiful,
their shapes a way of being helped
by water, wind. Even the plastic ones.

You don't have to be an old salt
to know that co-operation is the only axiom
that will carry you to the office and back.

I live in a Long Island of the mind
where hope bounces off the wave-tops
as they kick and break. Sometimes it's a sun

and sometimes wind. Always there's an edge,
a rough diplomacy of handshakes,
always a window and a woman's hand.

Mastery of the elements is a chimera
sighted only by the young. I should like
my mermaids to bake good pastry

and keep up their education, in return
for which good fortune I shall not set sail
for the blue of utter holiness, nor

put them to the expense of storm-shutters.
Wisdom just this side of fatuity
will put rings on our fingers

and keels to our passion. We shall love
the sea and the sand, and our children will
carry that ballast with them when they go.

Corfu

1.
Tired of swatting flies
I pull on my briefs
and stroll down the instep
of Pantokrator to a beach
gently smitten by
the one Ionian sea.

Not to be outdone
by Spiros and Xenophon
KEV has signed his name
on a broad cactus leaf
that rears from the cliff,
capitalising on nature
with his lapidary knife.

Further on down mermaids
are pasted all over the rocks,
cruciform and glad, each attended
by the soldier of the cream.
Idly riffling the sea
they won't read a single page.
They have renounced everything
for the art of being themselves.

2.
Rolling down her black
one-piece, slipping the clear water
over her legs, a young Greek stands
fronting the sea with new breasts
and its hard to know which perfection
most deserves the palm.

She swims. She lies prone
in the sun, then sits up
to hug her man, who pours
a little mineral water
over her head, beginning
at the fontanelle.

3.
Marble floors, pine ceilings,
our villa is by Berenson
out of Habitat... The sun
clicks on and off the cicadas'
grosse fugue, day-long, obscure
and raucous as the Greek for tears.

I fling a pan of cold water
over them at dusk,
hungry for a little peace.

A family of wild cats
plays under the olive trees
and begs for scraps, ready
to bolt at a raised voice
or adopt us as gods.
Angular and impolite, they swipe
titbits out of your hand
before your gesture is complete
or leap on the screechers
in the trees, turning down
the volume by a jot or tittle,
or by nothing at all.

4.
I'm here for scraps too—
honeydew and watermelon,
warm waves flapping at my thighs,
ouzo and lemonade with Jackie

by my ribs. She winds coloured
chiffon about her delectable skin,
oiled nightly at the tavern
with those scrumptious small sardines.
We'd eat each other, sometimes,
if we could, and chuck the heads
and tails of marriage to the cats ...

More fruit, more fruit
will be my deathbed cry.
One more bite of the pink
hacked from the watermelon's
unconscionable weight.
Then float me off
in the gondola, *liebestod* or no.

First Sailing

Imagine a thousand giant horseshoes
riveted together for good luck.

Imagine the decks stacked up like an in-tray,
the infant-class-drawing funnels

followed to the inch, the ton, sloping
back their ears and ready for the off.

Something is shaking the thing awake
under your feet and you race up on deck

where the wind off the Solent
flattens one side of you like a plank.

The handrail warps and judders; at a blast
of the last trump the whole ship

thinks itself into a greyhound tremble
and dreams away from the quay,

scouring a giant glass for seagulls
to scream in. The horizon turns slowly

round and proceeds to forget you
like relatives going home after a visit.

You have landed in luxury's hard lap.
Your wake stretches from here to nowhere.

Eldorado

As the band blew bubbly tunes from Rodgers and Hart
and streamers wobbled out and New York's democratic dockers
tolerantly pulled on gloves to heave at ropes, hoisting
us off with Marlon Brando shrugs, we backed out into

the Hudson's purple ice and headed south for St Thomas.
Just 48 hours saw us out of our Fruit of the Loom cotton
cladding and into the sun, the sights, the duty frees,
where young burnt-ochre beauties took in Washington's heads

and gave out liquors of a hyperbolic proof. Everywhere
we were met by tanned important men who dripped agencies,
chains and bangles, had a busy corner in the evolution
of time off. They sold watches, cameras, perfumes, rings;

their plaid coats and impeccable lightweight suits
were seen in morning conference with the Cruise Director's
influential face, his hair *en brosse*, his castling wrists
sketching percentages and itineraries. He was a big ship

and they were tugs, manoeuvring so much tonnage of wealth
down alleyways to bonded stores and local crafts,
to dazzly white hotels, where seafood writhed artistically
in tanks, and dancers limbo'd in a supple blaze of flesh.

Fourteen, sixteen, eighteen days we hopped the islands
happy as sandboys, oiling our bodies like moving parts.
All the empires had scattered memorabilia behind them
which made excellent backdrops for smiles. We focused quick

and shot them as they walked the plank, or sat in bars,
composing themselves in groups to fit the natural frame.
Bermuda's wall of surf tilted the ranked sunglasses
skywards, then swirled us clown-footedly into land.

The bombed-out streets of Port-au-Prince were black
as night, impenetrable as heads that turned indifferently
away, bent to their pots and battered Singers. Pristine
Grand Anse beach, Grenada, thundered softly to itself,

a blue-gold rondel painted on the dome of the eye
and sprung to three dimensions, not a ghost
of a balcony in sight, just girls in primary one-pieces
and a steel band's loosening of the music's tie.

Calypsos faded on Kingston's backtown roads, climbing
to clubs where age-old girls in demi-semi skirts, hot pants,
proposed I wine and dine them. Bacardi butted horns
with ice and Coke: Elvis rocked: a bevy of handsome stewards

came waltzing in to torment the girls, every last man
of them got up as subtly, slightly-whimsically gay
as angels in free-fall. They seemed to live in their own
dinky slipstream, cherubs whizzed right out of the frame.

The juke-box aspired to the condition of luv-luv-luv.
You want have me quick-slow, now, yes yes! Needless
to ask, since she had their collateral youth stripped
and banked before it knew it knew its ABC. I was the beau

of a Scottish hairdresser, ten years and a bit older
than me, who stayed in her snow-white slip through
thick and thin, however many brandy alexanders, fond
weakness, washed at the crumbling sandstone of her faith.

She undressed me one night in the cabin at St George.
Most amazing. She said I was hoarding myself up,
by which turnaround I think she meant to make amends
for my endlessly deferred wages of adoration.

Wait till we get to Havana, they used to tell me.
The *Copacabana*, huge scarlet fireflies, floorshows
you'll not believe. The girls who come and sit by you
at the movies will bring tears to your eyes.

I was just nineteen and ready for Eldorado,
a failure at school and therefore ripe for success.
The day we dropped anchor off Cuba gunfire
cracked out in the suburbs. Two crowded tenders

of bloods found themselves landed and caught
in a war. My one photo is of blurred figures
crouching behind a giant American sedan, *circa* 1951.
Fidel Castro was entering the city on his own terms

with not so much as nod to the Cruise Director,
whose busty assistants flew off to the upper decks
and officers-at-arms. Havana crackled there in
the sunlight, a not-quite-tuneable station after all.

—Me too. A much-loved chunky Laurel *Wings of the Dove*
and my sore eyes were inseparable for a week. It
still gripped and shook me in the morning sun
no matter how many times I'd seized the night before.

But the good times had to be moved on: Trinidad
and Curacao, Martinique's rumbustious mardi gras.
Fifty yards from where girls came inexorably swaying
like camels over rucked sand, cool fresh paw-paws

and pineapples somehow balanced on their heads,
a train ran over a sleeping fisherman, and far-off wails
mixed with the tired crash of the waves. Whole days
fell at my feet like fruit. When I took a shower, my trunk

was zoned and zippered like some allegory of state.
Soap-trails jetted down over the fabled Cartesian
latin of the mind, screwing up eyes too late
against the swelling honeycomb of pain . . .

Old-world English service and American cash: it was
the golden age of cruising, minting all pleasures on five
sentimental senses, which we snapped and proofed
cash on the nail. My love-life never quite matured.

It fogged in the camera, too much or too little art.
Ships' sweethearts ended up trailing the world's
discreetest perfumes and a frail gold tan,
their smiles just slightly out of reach of land.

On Fancy Dress Night the bloods went wild
then dived back into their sober bickering,
overtired and overspent, outlandish in all
the splendour of American accessory leisure wear.

The sky hung its head and the sea hunched up.
RMS MAURETANIA ploughed back to the diner on Twelfth
where blond and bovine waitresses, those Mrs Marlon
Brandos, sang out *Toasted English* to their stony chefs.

All at Sea

Half-way round the World Cruise
she seized every stitch of his clothes
and shoved them through the stateroom porthole,
silk bathrobes for Guam, Fifth Avenue suits
marching unsteadily to Yokahama,
Bermuda shorts for Brisbane, ties to Mindanao,
cargoes of monogrammed shirts for all Polynesia...
I thought: it's the young man's occupational hazard
spreading himself a little wider than he meant.

She booked all the long tours inland.
He took up residence on a bar stool
and became a student of ice cubes
and bartenders, the wealthiest men afloat,
dishing out liquor at the speed of light.

Senhouse Street

Effleurage, pétrissage, tapotement
are at her fingertips.
She unpicks frozen shoulder, wry
necks, exclamatory sciatic nerves.

Those recovering from accidents
to limbs are a light snowfall
on the field of her salon.
Certain types of arthritis also

respond. Her daughter Michelle
who is a qualified beautician
runs the sauna and trimnasium.
After five treatments the pain will go.

Prone, you have read the small print
on the framed certificate of
the Northern Institute of Massage
over and over, and the pain will go.

Five doors down the talky coach
to Maryport's burly tacklers prowls
among his voltages. He throws backs,
pollards the rank growth of nerves

in bodies running jarred on the field.
Alternative medicine has taken root
in Senhouse Street, in Queens Parade.
We are under the protection of a third eye,

of self-hypnosis and mantras on tapes.
Lie down under a warm blanket
and listen to the spools go round.
There are as many roads to health

as there are primary modes of rāg
and rules for their combination.
You can't have the morning in the evening.
Only at dusk will flutes creak to their nests.

Tap these lateral points with needles.
Let these scented fingers draw you out
in balmy parallels, as Krishna churns
the ocean for immortal youth. Who said

we can't reason by analogy? Certainly
not Laksmī, goddess of fortune, whose
pungent spirit rears up as Michelle
touches alight the trash-trail of a spark.

Road Movie

Shuffle up to the North Circular and look
for a gap in the great migration of cars.
Once through your tyres will thrum on the concrete
and tarmacadam like a Zen master eliding

the school of hard knocks into a momentary flutter
of the pulse. Here are the midlands, the up-and-down
lands colonised extensively by the big cats
of industry and parish pride. Push in the *Dire Straits*

cassette, point your camera at savannahs of unalterable
nouns. Autolatry stretches in all directions
framed in the heart-stopping discretions of dusk.
Tall sodium lamps droop their heads; fraternal

trucks thunder on by, or curl up for the night
behind rows of litter bins. Here comes a lithe
young hitch-hiker looking for the all-night ferry
to X, which just happens to be on your route.

She seems to have severed all relations with
the social sciences. Her only tense is now
expressed in one long syllable of hair.
What happens between here and 'The End' is up

to the lighting cameraman and the department
of reflexive grammar. As the ferry shrinks
and she semaphores with arms and hair you'll
gather the wits of the car and push off into

the uplifting misery of dawn, whose significance
comes at you like a madman with a cleaver
intent on separating the days of the week
into seven pillars of unalterable loss.

Younger Brother

Put in the ring
with someone two weights up
your reward is more sweets
and lowered expectations...

Wherever you go you trail
flash-forwards, like Yossarian.
Much of the war was fought
and all its strategies planned

before you got your olive drabs.
Is it not written that
variations must be on a theme?
A smile, a curve of the bum

that has gone ahead
on reconnaissance, whose flannel
trousers will infallibly be
cut down and handed on to you:

bred for cunning rather
than stamina, non-caster
of clouts, swaddled in
mother-love and olive oil,

blessed with Alyosha's smile
and only a baby grip
on the patrimony, which has
an eye out for another eye.

Therefore, oh my countrymen,
manually dextrous;
a bender of rules;
inward with dice;

immemorial bruise-bearer,
tale-bearer, first in line
for supplementary pocket money;
last name on the Xmas cards.

Der Gang Zum Liebchen

for David Lindley

Let stream the soul's desire
sang the baritone, sang the tenor.
And the accompanist's accompanist
came off the blocks to turn the pages
cueing in lip and throat and wrist
and silence, on a thousand stages.

O coo, you doves
O blow, you breezes
Give me life or give me death

Her hair is looped. She wears no rings.
She sits, like Patience, in the wings
neatly, nondescriptly dressed,
turns the page, then sits effaced.
In all this grand sublime of rage
she sits, she hides, she turns the page.

Will anxious feelings
stir in the immeasurable?
Ah, say but one word

Her very private hands and notions
keep their stations.
While Amour puffs his bulldog throat
and Pandar panders, note by note,
the river of her quiet runs
from nape to breast to broad white hands.

Begin
begin anew
your melodious plaint

Miss Person glides off swiftly. Now
a double, deep and gracious bow,
handshakes, smiles, applause, a tear.
Donated, in my case, to her
who guarantees the fol-de-rols
of English hearts and German souls.

Coming of Age in NW3

Unpredictable as sausage, Miss Gossek
ran the dusty old Victorian house,
its cats and furniture. Her ailing mother
shuffled somewhere in the gloom below
steep stairs; father's fine editions waned
to dust on alpine cupboards in the hall.
Once she'd been an artist's model, still
went off to previews, fancy nights in Bond
Street, reappearing sherry-eyed and cross.

I had a flat on the third floor, you took
the attic room above with one electric ring
foxing the walls, an easel, battered armatures,
living on soup and Phaidon's sexy colophon...

Remember, when we fought, how furious
your breast was to be touched, how anger
locked us in its lust? My arm shot back
outraged that pleasure was for getting
out of hate. One midnight you ran down
the stairs to hurl your masterpiece to smithereens
across my room. Bits of you were everywhere,
a plaster hailstorm rattling round my books...
Naked as Spartans, who would stoop
to cultivate the bourgeois arts of peace..?

Pather Panchali made me weep, so did
the freeze-frame on *Four Hundred Blows*
but I kept my young man's powder dry.

The Waverer

It's taken me twenty years to learn to see
Christmas through your panic-stricken eye.

Each December you are a hunted deer.
The dogs have names like money and good cheer

and close in on you as you circle round
togetherness's jolly hunting ground.

Noli me tangere ... Not a bit
heeded. Oh daughter-of-the-house-that-split

don't take off through that wood again. The sons
who trail you now won't carry guns

but sixpacks, noisy records, an art calendar
to plot their tongue-tied need of you next year.

Those Vuillard inscapes, and those Cézanne pines
are subtle, manageable pains....?

I've planted tiny candles on the boughs.
If you must run away, dear, run to us.

The Woman Who Wouldn't Sit Down

Up at dawn to propitiate
the coffee god, your grateful throat
heads for the Derwent's kindly light

whose Steiner School of gradual curves
and glimmering pastoral gently lags
by root and mill, while our two dogs

accelerate across the fields
or bristle up, bracing themselves
against a running sea of smells.

Five solemn ducklings are on tow;
a heron crashes from a bough;
the cows are deep in how to chew

thoughtfully ... Their sides display
the abstract lesson for today,
how time becomes geography.

You walk for miles and miles, come back
to find us milksops half awake,
face down in our breakfast tack.

So much for prologue. Then the long
slow heart-to-heart with space ... form
... that subtle song

of almost-utterance, as you coax
an alphabet from untold facts ...
O tempera, O melted wax

chaotic as the nursery, where you try
old newsprint on the half-closed eye
of innocent posterity.

At six, or thereabouts, we might just eat.
This arty household's always late...
A colloquy, a cigarette

but even then you won't sit still.
You'll walk, or work, or worry, till
your legs give out. Eventually, head to tail

(after the bathroom   hail! farewell)

you sigh one last big sigh, your face
composed, your paws at peace,
dreaming through the long tall grass...

Hypnos

for Heidi Birck

The sculptor has made me a little god,
Hypnos, god of sleep, whose one wing
broods over the shelf where I put him

by Gilchrist's angel-smothered Blake,
those ruined, hand-sewn spines
of Steele and Pope, ivied now in dust

that somehow clings through every move
and mortgage. He has a cherub's fat
young face, full of the new bread

of himself, open to suggestion
as the martyred heads of infants
cut down neatly on their desks

for the midday nap. The other wing
was lost by history. His shut lids
seal the birth of two faint smiles.

You made him way out west, where east
comes scudding under the Golden Gate
its pilot safe and well, and fast asleep.

The Perfect Uncle

Is very bald and not altogether well-tempered.
His glasses flash like a heliograph, and what
he signals is not necessarily peaceful or clear.

A bowls addict, he cultivated biasses against boredom,
rolling his arguments at you from round the pillar
of his pint. When he was on the up and up

he grew perfect tomatoes in lieu of a dead child
and treated me to more rides and Italian ice-cream
than the heat in my tongue could ever quench.

Given the OBE for services to the Royal Train
this one-time wheel-tapper from Swindon
cultivated the good life in the dreary suburbs

of south London, alas. He wished Labour well
and all test selectors in another line of business.
I think choler drove every last hair out of his head.

Now, watching him struggle comically for words
in a hospital bed, himself versus himself,
the woods of his kindness glide in and topple

all about the kempt lawn of my heart.

Death of a Bird

He's like a bird himself: small
marbled eyes, a beaky nose, tall
cliffs of silence under all he says.
Two sons, three daughters drew no praise
from him. Their mother took them off
to Canada to miss the war
and he was left non-combatant, a pure
and bitter gruffness all he had
to service buried powerlines. The bad
times over, when they trickled back
at intervals, with accents full of luck,
his silence deepened. The eldest son
went mad, the daughters, cursed at, flung
themselves at pleasure all the more.
His bony face slammed shut.

In Norfolk, where the wind can chide
a landscape in a single stride
he came to rest
with rooks and rain, a garden fat with best
potatoes, carrots, beans; an ailing wife
plumping a narrow afterlife
into a lifetime's nap; and in a cage
a budgie, brightly coloured. When it died
it stuck its stiff feet out, and Harry cried.

Eclogue: Clerk of the Weather

If solitude, or fear, or pain, or grief,
Should be thy portion ... (*Tintern Abbey*)

for Pamela Woof

A. The nut-brown maid of Grasmere plays
    amanuensis to the lays
    of William and the weather, which,
    entire unto itself, is rich
    in characters, and scenes, and plots,
    monumental rorschach blots
    streaming over Helm Crag, bowed
    in great long paragraphs of cloud
    or sounding quiet midnight's noon
    with all the quarters of the moon.

B. Aye, Dorothy, poor lass. Was her
    twinned up a poet's character,
    two poets, mebbe. Then she fell
    back on the thinkin of hersel
    and Lord knows but the weather turned.
    Naebiddy knows what she learned—
    days and nights as strange to her
    as to the fust Mrs Rochester.
    Up in her room she twitched, she crowed
    like some old gipsy on the road.

A. *The moonlight lay upon the hills—*

B. —like snaw. Aye. Pretty stuff.
    It sells the beuks, and's true enough.
    But what came down in her distress?
    *My own thoughts are a wilderness
       not pierceable by any power.
    I have fought and fretted and striven—
       and am here beside the fire.*
    Where once all nature was lawgiver
    she sees the *naked seed-pods shiver.*

A. Jean-Jacques, maybe, was not so clever
in banishing the Fall? For they
lacked reasons for mortality
and fallings-off, and said so in
great heartfelt bursts of poetry
which found scant room for death or sin
in Grasmere's tolerable Eden.

B. William was God, and mebbe too
he was the serpent.

A.   Incest?

B.   Pooh!
But love—love is its own taboo,
festering slowly on the stem.
The naked seed-pods: what of them?
You'd think in getting down the shrill
raw beauty of a daffodil
they'd said it once and once for all ...

A. Nay. Lucy played in sun and shower—

B. He struck her dead, made death a flower
that splits the rocks. Remember when
they laid down in their graves an hour
and went together home again?
She died, in life, for love. Just that
sings through her brief magnificat.
One note she held, like that last leaf
she speaks of, pure atomic grief
that whirls and spins perpetually
in the gaunt socket of the tree.

A. If they'd had modern drugs—

B.   Aye, give
or take an epoch, she might live
as we do, and have dosed her heart
with the black drop of modern art;
conned the dream that she was in
and smote it with an aspirin ...

A. We love a mystery—such bliss
   in tortuous analysis!
   But there's no need. She aged, and fell
   into disease. She grew unwell.

B. Unsomething, aye: unhinged, unmanned,
   nor never wore a wedding band
   again. *News—I must seek for news*
   she says. There is none. She is bruised
   to silence, soon to pass on down
   to her dear Godchild, one green gown.

A. *A mind o'erthrown—*

B.   Is Babylon
   in ruins. And we know no more
   than that affecting metaphor.
   The wild lights in her eyes died down
   to solitude, and fear, and pain
   within a babby's bonnet pent.
   The Wye ran on, magnificent,
   unchanging. All the words were spent
   and bought her a last quiet place
   to know the Bedlam of her face,
   fronting the worst that time had done
   and all the elements, but one.

Rydal Water, Winter

Some dynasty has squatted down
politely on its hams
and taken up the thought of home
around these pale, phantasmal things,
a lake solid with ghostly colour
drypoints of the dryest silver.

Last night's frost sits poised to go.
A muted, misty brightness
doubles up each hill, each tree
into a dream, a real completeness
cupped in winter's palm
as in a weightless Chinese poem.

Such emblems of departed powers:
poor Col, poor Lamb, poor Dorothy.
In Rydal's quiet book of hours
Dame Nature writes her litany
of forms and signs, so piercing-sad
dusk bows its dark north-country head.

And like a girl in any mirror
who skates on past self-love
seeing such vistas to adore
as earth will hatch reversals of
we tremble, and the mirror flares,
seeding the first faint shiver of stars.

Nicola
for Tim and Liz

In eighteen months she has grown
to fit her rompers—perfectly.
The soft hair too has started
on its journey down her back.
When it's two feet long
she will have a small museum
of Lilliputian china in her room
and O-levels for every three inches.
Meanwhile she is all-coloured and ignorant,
padded up against damage in transit,
shoving a Sibyl's head up close
against the bending cheekbone
of her mother's smile.

And all this in The Nab
where Quince and Hartley dreamt of fame,
eating the young pink char from Rydal,
learning first how hard it was
just to wake up to the light on the lake.

To a Pink Dress

after Gautier's *A une robe rose*

How I like you in that dress
which half-undresses you so well,
baring your pagan arms' soft zeal,
liaising with your nakedness.

Sharp as the wing-flash of a bee
cool as the labyrinth of a rose
the silk's delicious artistry
on hip and breastbone overflows.

Who made it, where's the label,
what old sempstress dreamed a robe to think
itself awake in perfect pink
haunting the column of your throat?

Did you steal colour from the dawn
one morning, or from Venus' shell,
or from the hint of your own nipple
bursting from its immortelle?

Or is the stuff dyed in the core
of modesty? Ah no! I guess
you've modelled twenty times before
and know the splendour of your flesh.

And these pink folds and slashes are
the mutes of love, its deep, dumb wink,
the famished lips of my desire
that robes you in heartbreaking pink.

Boaz and Ruth

after Hugo's *Booz Endormi*

Boaz laid down in his own exhaustion.
He'd threshed all day on a dusty floor
then made his bed in the open air
sacked in sleep, at his usual station.

The old man's land was good, his barley
wheat and rye flooded everywhere.
Though rich, he was known to be quite fair.
His forge, his mill worked late and early.

His beard ran white as an April beck.
His sheaves were generous to a fault.
When the gleaners had gathered to a halt
'Let some ears fall on purpose,' he said.

An upright man: no wiles, no front,
candid, honest, dressed in white linen,
honoured by all; to those in want
his sacks of grain were a public fountain.

Gaffer, confessor, widower, diviner;
generous, but not for public show.
Women liked him, and told him so—
young men are fine, but the old are finer.

A man past his prime bends low to the source;
the young think passion's all in all,
cupping the days, seeing light gall;
an old man's lust lights on remorse.

Boaz lay quiet; in the cool of the meadow
the workers slept by old mill-stones
spilling their darkness like ancient ruins.
This all happened a long time ago

when Israel's chief was a living god;
they wandered the land, living in tents,
seeing signs, scared stiff by giants
printing an earth still soft from the flood.

   * * *

Like Jacob, like Judith, Boaz lies
shut fast beneath a gate of stars:
a dream came dropping from high dark bars
to station itself before his eyes.

And the dream told Boaz an oak tree sprang
out of his body into the sky;
the people climbed up in an endless chain
from a king to a wounded deity.

And Boaz, astonished, softly said
'How can such issue stem from me?
My years add score to score, indeed
I have no son, and my wife's long dead.

An age has passed since she quit my bed
to sleep in yours, O Lord! Yet still
I sense her life in mine, I feel
that she's half living and I'm half dead...

A race to be born of me? Un—
say it: how can the old fruit more?
Young, it's a different story—the door
of desire lies open night and day—

but the old must tremble, a birch in winter;
I am weak, alone; these eyes grow dark;
my soul bends low towards its mark
as a thirsty ox leans to clear water.'

Thus spoke Boaz, compelled by a dream,
his sleep-drowned eyes fixed fast on God;
knowing no more that a woman stood
at his side than a rock can know the stream.

   * * *

For while he slept the Moabite, Ruth
stole naked to him in the night
hoping, though chaste, she knew not what;
sank at his feet, a living swath

cut and commanded by God. She knew
nothing of this; Boaz knew less.
Hushed asphodels shook their abyss
of perfume down the heavenly blue.

Boaz' breath forms an element
among these others, the becks, the moss;
it was the year's most perfect month;
lilies starred the body of grass.

Ruth lay still; Boaz slept on;
sheep-bells quavered; all earth was dark;
beneficence dropped from heaven's great arc;
it was the hour of the thirsty lion.

Everything slept, in Ur, Jerimadeth;
stars enamelled the vast of sky;
a sickle moon curved low in the fosse
of night's last darkness. Motionless

Ruth, tranced in veils, half wakes, half stirs.
What god, what reaper of endless summer
had thrown away his scythe, to glimmer
carelessly in a field of stars?

Outcast

after De Béranger's *Le Vieux Vagabond*

for Derek Mahon

In this ditch I'll do a bunk.
I'm tireder than a prozzy's leg.
The world will think me good and drunk.
It would—and walk on with its dog
eyes averted. Some throw pence,
others hurry off to play.
Some piss their kindness at the fence.
Okay, I don't need you to die.

I think I'll settle it right here
for lack of birthdays, not of grub.
No-one's starving any more;
they steer by giro to the pub.
I'd thought I'd snuff it in white sheets
but there's a waiting list for those
so it'll have to be the streets
where I was born, and nearly froze.

They kicked me out of school. I tried
to learn a trade from older blokes.
They fetched their boot to my backside.
'Go on the dole, like other folks—
there's not enough for us.' The rich
were big, as always, with advice.
I combed their dustbins, found my niche
in pigsties, and grew weather-wise.

I could've thieved; I could've been
one of the boot-boys, hell for leather,
carving up pedestrian
wage-earners and their pious blether.
But no: I only stuffed my face
with fallers and a bit of sun.
They shoved me in a busy place
for loitering; or moved me on.

What country ever owned a tramp?
Am I supposed to stand and cheer
when politicians rub the lamp
and blow the genie more hot air?
What's it to me if firms grow fat
and Shell, BP and ICI
sleep sounder than Jehosephat?
Good luck. I don't need them to die.

The faces frown; they know my type.
Why bring me up to bring me down
a common, stinking guttersnipe
here on the wrong side of the town?
Ah, screw the lot of you! You've not
the honesty to tell a lie
has got you all you've ever got.
Don't tell me. I know how to die.

There's something in this pauper's bed:
it runs to vetch, and daisy-fret.
Cow-parsley nods above my head
the only requiem I'll get.
The beetles are in solemn black.
There's holy water right nearby.
I'll just get straighter on my back.
You need a little warmth to die.

Larkin's Dead

A tall man, with thick specs.
No beauty much of face.
The alto voice erects
his doleful time and place:

England, late on, stuck
for policy, run out
of things to shout about,
money, time, and luck.

Back in the pavilion
he wasn't heard to say
'I could've made a million.'
He packed his bat away

neatly—he always did—
and walked off for his bus,
not himself, exactly,
and not exactly us.

We had a good time, once—
a woman, an idea.
Such transitory stunts
he thought small, bitter beer.

Which was his loss. Still
it flung him certain rights
to play the old Old Bill
on lost and lonely nights

collaring deception,
duffing up pretence,
charging all conception
with lethal lack of sense.

Here it was, loitering
with intent to intend
a queasy reconnoitring
of love, whose latter end

was clear in its first yodel
so therefore why begin?
Write *finis* on the cradle;
baptise the mannekin

with sundry cures for colics,
likewise a love of jazz
and hope his little frolic's
more gin than Vichyssoise . . .

And good luck to him. He
said true, sad, funny things.
Let Hull inter the body
We've his imaginings.

Library

Young girls paw softly at the issue desk;
and silent men in suits, whose glasses trap
the light, make fish mouths at necessity.
In these waxed rooms all days and postures
sediment; a week-old scream looks like
a Roman after-dinner speech.
Sometimes a travelling shark gets through
to sieve the lower stacks. A flurry of
printers' mud: and hung on turning light
by ponderous two-way exit doors
there spins the slippery, unforgiving text.

Learning the Cello

There is much to be learned. It is all
hard and compelling. I write this in honour
of my father, bootblack, pantryboy, plumber
who read Dumas under the bedclothes, tall
at a penny candle, quartered the New Forest
on his Brough (my sainted mother up behind),
loved dancing and billiards and was sometimes kind
to the flaming of his nearest and dearest.
'That music's gloomy!' I can hear him say
who adored families not to agree
and sleep: 'like eating a rasher of wind!'
As you did, oh my father, at the end.
My wrist gives. I must learn to play.

Pub

In the dark cabin of the pub
where oak has fetched up like a moth
your empty glass still stood
in its pegnoir of froth

severe and dimpled. Yes she's gone
off home to be alone (it said)
which is a more profitable burden
than you and the starlight in your head.

The temple of the empty glass.
The publican with classic taste.
The glimmering T-shirts' billets doux.
The waste, the waste.

More Bagatelles

1.
Hers the statement
under the knitwear, the globe
empurpled in designer jeans.

No use to call in
the crack regiment of *isms*.
She commands the high ground.
She is dug fast into her wrist, her smile.

2.
Consider the wicked
yin of the cello,
how it yearns for
the addition of the bow.
I tell you, in a decent world
culture wouldn't be allowed.

3.
What's your poison
pal? I'd have to say books,
those Age of Reason jobs...
Such fine receipts
set drowning in the floury page!

4.
A happy Frankenthaler
makes her want to kiss.
Perhaps it will sustain us.
This is only the first room
and we have many styles to go.

5.
Somehow the books and the girls
recur, the childish pleasure
of effs for esses sets
me off up the aisle
on the arm of printed love.

Tree Heads

The great tree heads are on the move again.
They wear their brains on the outside
agreeing with everything in sight.

Imagine ignorance on that scale! Fancy
not knowing a cliché to look down on!

Olive and Autumn

A day of huge techtonic skies
goes piling on past every ridge.
Whirly whirly under our town bridge
the river flattens, reifies

writing impeccable physics on
its much-medallioned back,
a chic and brainy organon
where systems form and melt and break . . .

like you, Olive, bouncing down
high street in your purple salopettes
(with big white spots)

tumbling all about the town
executing perfect stops
at babies, boyfriends, coffee shops.

Seven Smells

1. BACON
Up on its points,
a ballet dancer
who also knows
how to do the splits,
the pig wallops the air
with retroactive funerary splendour.

2. FRUIT
A sea and a wood
joined in holy matrimony.
Naked on the day-bed
of your teeth
your mouth just comes and comes.

3. COFFEE
Miss Styx
sways down the catwalk
straight at you, narcolepsis
on the instalment plan,
in a little black number
that will cost the earth.

4. NEW BREAD
Wants elbow-room,
filling up the house
like a burst pipe...
or the pipe of Pan.
O for the wings,
the do-it-yourself Blakean sublime!

5. DUST AFTER LIGHT RAIN
Prickles the nose,
a fishbone
in meaning's fishy throat.
Aux armes, Proust . . . This one
wrinkles with indefinition,
turns lights to amber,
sows the pavements
crop-deep in nothing.

6. CUT GRASS
Cantilena
melodies for violins,
you know, the ones that bring
tears to your eyes,
little earthquakes in your speech.
You could repent, or cut your wrist.
You could ascend a little, like the dew.

7. SKIN
Aha!
the talc-maker's ball
the skater's waltz
the hunt by day
the eye's masseuse.

I cease, therefore I exist.

You could pull
it over your shanks
and hibernate in this.

Da Capo

after Petronius

She has muddied her face with tears
and barred it with crossover wrists.
She is hair from top to bottom.
The wind in her shoulders

blows her down into the tomb
where his corpse lies amid tokens
of honour and respect. Its limbs
have gone hard already, hard and small,

as though this were a replica
in some unknown material.
The likeness is such
she punishes her face.

The maid cries too. They work
their grief together, for him,
the late master and husband,
who gives off a plaque of cold.

Nothing will bring them out alive,
not well-wishers or friends.
They brush off instances.
Their virtue is terrifying.

It reaches up to a soldier
out in the sun who guards
the remainders on crosses.
It's a bad job, watching

the exemplary dead, looking out
for relatives with their prayers
and spades. Even the birds
make detours round this place.

A noise that snores and saws; the flip
of wind in a dead latch of hair.
He climbs down underground, wine and meat
in hand. Two apparitions beat

their breasts. It's like a play,
this fright between them in the dark.
He eats, he makes a dumbshow
of his good intentions, tempting

the starving maid with pungent wine.
The other is a woman steeped
in mid-life beauty, ruffling her feathers
over a high nest of bone.

Weird ... and the fact weird too
that grief is comely, and the flesh-stump
knows what cannot be borne
and overpowers liberality of mind.

This is flatly unspeakable.
It flares in the stink of his meat,
settles in the chime of a bottle on stone.
Revolt stirs in his tunic

and she knows it, the maid knows it,
the dead man and the crucified
tell them all what it feels like
to pitch into the dark.

Her lips bounce off the one
and are devoured by the other,
for a corpse is potent
more ways than the coroner knows.

At night the soldier comes back.
The maid is their only priest
giggling in a far corner. The pomp
of widows weeds makes up a bed.

Scrambling to his dawn watch
the soldier finds an empty cross
and runs wildly back to the woman
sleeping soundly in the tomb.

The punishment is death by restitution,
his body for the body gone. She
cannot believe it, her terror throbs
operatically off the dripping walls.

As the light grows, so does her fear.
There's a body just six feet away—
and who's to poke their face up close
at a thing humped foxwise on a cross?

The living husband manhandles
the dead one awkwardly into place.
So the sun comes up on seven bodies.
So the woman from Ephesus

is enrolled in the long story
of how men look at women,
sidling up with a shocked giggle,
as well they might, to love.

Byron's Bedroom

'She was younger than me, with her hands perpetually
down his trousers, and his head just followed his balls'
said the deserted wife in a voice not at home with her own
brazen diction. 'He had a coronary out of the blue at 36.
That started it all. Survived, and saw himself out the door
into green pastures. What can you do?' Quivering at me
her quality-cut blonde hair shook out intimacies over
the tea-cups of Newstead Abbey, courting my interest in
a manner half-remembered from the pyhrric 'fifties. 'I'd
understand it if we'd been unhappy, but we weren't. We liked
each other. It was great.' A bell boomed and a suited matron
entered at a trot. 'This way for the tour of Byron's Bedroom.'

The irony fell pat, not meeting the case of her eyes following
me round the bar that night or buying halves between literary
chat (the case of Plath . . .). Inheriting his title, undergraduate
Byron had a coronet put on each high corner of his four-poster,
'seen, it is thought,' says our sly guide, 'by more than one
lady from below.' I wonder what the runaway husband has on his,
assuming he's withstood that mid-life shock; how many half-
read books and shiny pills announce her sad majority?

I like Byron—getting up at midday, lording it with his pistols,
obliging importunate ladies, blackening sovereigns, drinking
and swimming till dawn sends him stumbling to cold saintly linen . . .
He's a whole Russian novel avant le lettre (as Russian letters
quickly knew) complete with maimed foot, gothic pets, natural
hatreds, a frozen steppe of mother-love on which to spur desire.
You might say his balls were synoptic, classical ballocks indeed
gassing away like translators inside their little booths while
the big powers drew up stony agendas. Pleasure wants accords,
détente; money fiddles its papers; decency won't budge that
standing army of reproach. What's to be done about the
squanderers, licit-illicit needs brightening and dying
like the smell of paint? Everyone wants pain on their own

terms, absolute integrity of the borders, no taxes on the logic
of self-love. The psychic rich pay up and the poor float
shares in disillusion, raising small sums on their wounds.

Between Byron and the blond sorrow hugs its mattress,
dry ticking under the giddy stripes. You would think
by this time there'd be some agreed wisdom to insinuate
in party walls, some commonsense fibre lagging the roof
against a frost of boredom, a blind for those inordinate
windows facing south... Where shall they look? Out on the lawn
is only an Asia of recurrence mapped in dun.

Verses

1. NEW ELIZABETHAN
Sir Norman Hartnell is my name
the Higher Clothing is my game.
I've dressed the Queen for years and years
in frocks that lie too deep for tears.

2. VICTORIANA
You can get off on pain.
Freud destroys Mill.
The felicific calculus
won't come again.

That leaves Darwin
gentlest of men
Virgil to everyone's
Everyman.

3. SEMIOTICS
'You're great, you're great' she whispered
into my proximate ear.
She'd a first in Psycho-linguistics
and a tell-tale teddy bear.

4. LONG LAND
The long land stretches out
thumped at by seas.
From one we tout
the other's quiddities.

That much for wisdom—depthless,
sad, canonical.
A change of scene... No more, no less,
God help us all.

5. THE BLACK HOTEL
It's 2a.m. in a large hotel.
Trade & Industry is summoned
to the PM's suite and given hell.

Imagine the walk along the hall.
Imagine the aides, mopping and mowing.
Imagine the large Shakespearian fall:
Stand not upon the order of your going...

Trade & Industry has faltered
managed too little and managed too much.
Trade & Industry has paltered
and the story's rich

bubbling the paint on editorials...

Lust and power, power and lust
locked in a smidgeon of sleepydust.

6. POETRY READING
The large much-educated lady
in her bright red suit
drops words into a made lake
of attention.
                Inches
to my right a baby snores
and farts at the breast.
The breast is bare. One
of those modern mothers
who thinks that life should be
allowed to go on anywhere.

7. BIRTHDAY BOY

Good Lord! Myfanwy! Philip! Kingers!
   Osbert! Sparrow! Mulinex!
Oh my stars, here's the Kings Singers
   pastiching select collects!

Up Parnassus grunt the twee ones
   down the High the Oxbridge stag
practises unerring re-runs
   of the nurs'ry: death in drag!

Windy dons of dereliction
   fruity vintners of the plough
connoisseurs of campest diction
   take him to your bosoms now.

8. GALLEY SLAVE

The editor cuts my quotes,
my apercus, to fit
a little poetry in
among the cookery books
and travellers in prose.
Upmarket but downpage
singers stand shorn
of all but their names
thrones and dominions.

I shall know the score
in heaven, legless
at the thrash on Helicon.

It's All Right, Ma, I'm Only Sighin'

Here it is, by Red Star
electric red, the new guitar

sitting in a long, discreet
coffin-coloured carrying case

all the way by night mail
from West Ealing to Carlisle

where dads relieve the BR porters
of their homing Christmas daughters

(sheepskin-coated, he, and she
in something good by Liberty).

Hit those solos, bend the notes
put a penny on the rates

by which we subsidise the arts
and freshen up our broken hearts.

My girl's gone. I'm a mess.
Took off in her ra-ra dress.

It's serious, it's criminal
she took her lips, she took her smile.

I'm me she said, and wept and laughed
snatched up Mary Wollstonecraft

several Dory Previn tapes
Renoired all her wondrous shapes

out to the car, made a mouth
at history, and drove off south.

Here she is, by Red Star
electric red, my new guitar.